RU

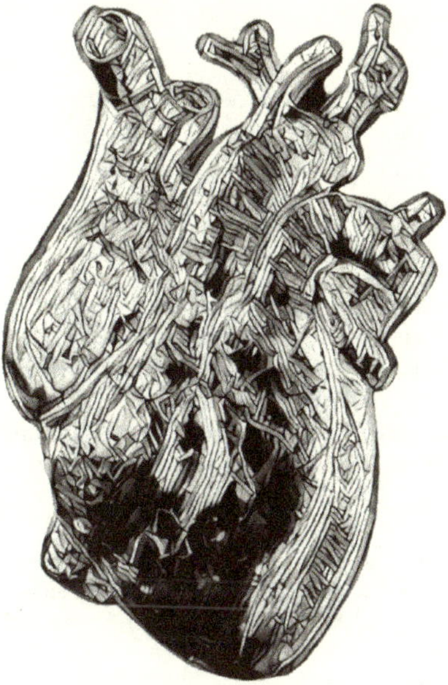

2732 PRISMS OF LOVE-STAINED LIGHT

a collage essay

PUBLISHED BY THE JAR WRITERS' COLLECTIVE

Brisbane & Sydney, Australia
Baltimore, MD, United States of America

ISBN 978-0-6486706-4-3
eISBN 978-0-6486706-9-8

First published globally, 2021

Edited by Jodi Cleghorn
Cover and Internal Design by The Booktress
Fonts: A Day Without Sun, ZetaFonts via Canva

www.thejarwriterscollective.com
info@thejarwriterscollective.com

There are moments in our lives,
There are moments in a day,
When we seem to see beyond the usual.
Such are the moments of our greatest happiness.
Such are the moments of our greatest wisdom.

-Robert Henri

CONTENTS

THE GLASS THAT IS ALL AROUND ME **1**
LEAD 9
ORANGE 15
RED 19

THE GLASS THAT HOLDS THE BRANDY **25**
STONE 29
SAND 37
ASH 45

THE GLASS THAT STARR CARRIES AWAY **49**
GREEN 55
BLUE 61
SAND, ASH, STONE, FIRE 67

THE GLASS THAT CARRIES MEGS AWAY **83**

ABOUT RUS VANWESTERVELT 91
ABOUT PRISMS & THE COLLAGE ESSAY 92
THE JAR WRITERS' COLLECTIVE 94

To You, staring into the mirror,
wondering what lies beyond the images of all
that has been placed before you,
but never within you.

To You, who embraces both
the spirit within and the spirit around you.

To You, who seeks not knowledge but Truth
through Faith in the unknown.
The unnamed.
The Universal Truth.

To You, the Embodiment:
Love.

There Is Always A Clearing

There is always a clearing.
I discovered this long after you had passed,
Where, in the absence of light I imagined the night
Opening its pitch-black door just right — ajar
For eyes like mine that yearned for hope, promise,
Love.
And there you were — are — still to this same night,
Where we wait to watch the meteors light the sky
For those who yearn to see the light,
Believe in the clearing (*there is always a clearing*)
That kindles promises bright.

~Rus VanWestervelt

THE GLASS THAT IS ALL AROUND ME

The winds have moved on, and now the sleet is nothing more than the sound of falling grains of sand on the abandoned slide and swing set in the grounds beyond. The fallen trees protrude deeply into my sacred space. The once-adored stained-glass window-walls lie around me in shards of greens, blues, yellows and reds; a prism-laced minefield of broken dreams and shattered hopes. The dark night mutes its colors, so nothing but flashes of full moon effulgence – captured in dew-drop bubbles of melting ice – light the remnants of a Christ crucified, a wooden cross splintered, and a band of disciples kneeling, falling, ululating all around my feet.

"*Jesus*," I whisper.

Fighting a fever that is pushing 102 degrees, I'm hesitant to step in any direction, afraid of desecrating the shards of Christ, as much as worrying about cutting my feet. Fear finds me in all directions, in all ways.

I stand in an absence of space to move, to think, to breathe.

This abandoned church, remade as a one-room schoolhouse, and now my temporary residence in Sherborn, Massachusetts, found me early one November evening as I searched for a space to write. I had made the long trek up 95, wearing out mixed tapes of everything from The Eagles to The Beatles to Elton John. The songs were as reflective as they were energizing, making the eight-hour trip pass by with as few stops as possible. I was on the run, desperately seeking salvation on the pages of my first novel: a psychological horror story set between the shores of Chesapeake Bay and an imagined small town just southwest of Natick. While I hoped Sherborn would serve as a haven following the death of my father, this tiny stone dwelling had become a sanctuary for me and my writing struggle. It sat some distance from the main farmhouse. Between stood Starr Sedgwick's studio: a barn converted into a stained-glass artist's workshop.

Starr met me at the long driveway when I showed up to sign the short-term rental agreement. He told me to leave my packed car where it was, and led me on a walking tour of the property.

He was much taller than me, and his long gait made me nearly have to run to keep up with him. Brown curls escaped the rim of the brown knit cap he wore (I later learned it was a permanent fixture regardless of the weather), and his work-soiled clothes hung off of him as if he had lost a lot of weight, or just enjoyed the loose-fit comfort look now fashionable in the early 90's. His whole appearance was a stark contrast to my husky build camouflaged in a crimson argyle sweater, khakis, and marginally scuffed burgundy penny loafers.

The farmhouse was built in the early 1830s; the church soon followed and served as one of Sherborn's first houses of worship. Somewhere just prior to the turn of the twentieth century, the barn, where Starr had stopped, was constructed in three days by his ancestors and local parishioners, happy and eager to do anything for the Sedgwick family.

"You would have fit right in with the Sedgwicks," said Starr, as we stood in front of the barn. "A solid bunch of writers and editors when all of this was being built. I imagine there's still some of their energy here for ya to tap into."

He stepped up to the main door and grabbed the edge with his fingers, sliding it to the left to reveal a cascade of natural light falling through a glass ceiling nearly invisible from where we stood.

"This is my first home," he said. "Sometimes I have a meal or two with Megs over there at the house." He thumbed to his right, indicating the large white structure. "I know you get it, though, you being a writer and everything. We artists. We just get in our zone. There are days when nothing outside of these old wooden walls exists for me."

I nodded to Starr, still staring inside, where seven large worktables, with projects in varying stages of progress, lined the inner perimeter of the barn. In the far-right corner of the studio, a few tables had been pushed together for a larger project. It carried a different energy; the space felt more cared for. An ancient piece of dogwood, maybe nine feet tall, leaned in the corner, with a rosary hanging from a nail about eye level.

"Funny," Starr said, walking to a repository of his tools at the center of the studio: grinders, worn pliers, soldering irons, lead, and of course, sheets of glass in varying hues, sizes, and shapes. From an outsider's perspective, it was chaotic; yet, I guessed every tool, every shard of glass, every piece of lead, was in its rightful place and had a purpose. It would all have an eventual home in a work of art.

"You take any of the elements – sand, ash, limestone – solid as can be. Concrete. Intended for just one job. Everything changes when you add energy."

His eyes lit up and I realized he was talking about the process of making glass.

"That energy is a fire of 2,732 degrees. In that heat, the opaque becomes transparent. Sand, ash, and limestone become glass."

Transformation, I thought. *Evolution*. Endless possibility.

"You make a living out of stained glass?" I asked, suddenly regretting it. How many times had I winced when asked the same question about being a writer?

"I get by." Then he smiled. "Just won a job redoing all the stained glass in the state buildings, including the Capitol. I keep telling Megs we don't need to be renting that old church anymore, but she can't help but be interested in the people it attracts."

"I got the feeling when I called about the ad she had – I don't know how to really say it."

"That she had been waiting for you?"

I looked up at Starr and nodded. "Something like that."

Starr laughed and closed the barn door. "Bring her some brandy tonight and let her talk. She has some stories to tell. That's all I'll say. Now for the church." He pointed to the stone structure on the hill. "Let's see if it likes you as much as you might like it."

I followed Starr along the gravel path, wondering how many times local parishioners had taken the same walk on Sunday mornings for some fellowship and prayer. While the front lawn of the church remained clear, it was surrounded by tired oaks with sagging branches pleading for an offering. On this early November day, most of the autumnal hues had already fallen, covering the ground like a tattered and worn quilt, once vibrant with life and color.

Just below the eastern side of the church, about 500 feet away on a leveled pasture, stood long-abandoned swings and a slide, longing for the children who once played on them daily.

Starr walked up the stone steps, dead leaves crunching under his boots, and opened the door under the great stone gateway. I couldn't see any lock, and as if to read my mind, Starr said, "We got a deadbolt on the inside, but you won't have any worries up here. Megs calls it God's country. I call it a place where people are still nice to each other and respect your space."

"Maybe they are close to the same thing," I offered, following him inside.

A kaleidoscope of color filled the great space as light filtered through the stained-glass windows on the west side of the room. They towered from floor to ceiling in wide columns, populated by disciples looking toward the back of the church, where the crucifixion of Christ filled the entire wall in eminent vibrancy.

I felt a lot of things: Reverence. Fear. Holiness. Spirituality.

And something else.

"The space in this great room is what called me to be an artist," Starr said, watching me try to reconcile the beauty of the glass with whatever was going on deeper within me. "Christ and his chromatic buddies were my first teachers in the art of color and glass."

Starr smiled, as if he had just introduced me to his greatest mentors from grade school.

"All original glass to this day. When the church closed and they converted it into a schoolhouse, they took the pews and converted the sacristy to a bedroom and bathroom, for the teacher. Over there to the right of the altar."

I couldn't see it, but I didn't doubt him.

"To the left where the pipe organ used to be," he said, pointing. "That's now the kitchen."

"It's all I need," I said under my breath, wondering if I would be able to leave when the book was finished.

"Cycles, man. You'll hear it from Megs. She knows. She

went here when it was a school. Now it's for people like you and me. When we're gone, it'll be something new for someone else. Cycles."

I could see where the pews had been fastened to the floorboards, and I envisioned the parishioners shifting their weight halfway through the homily, children wriggling and stretching, asking how much longer. The hushes. The flipping of pages in Psalms. The sounds of hymns rising.

"Megs said you didn't have any furniture with you, so I'm going to pull a few things out of the farmhouse to set you up. We even have a pew or two that are serviceable as couches with a few pillows. It won't be anything to write home about, but it will get you through."

I walked up to the altar and let the colors catching the setting sun wash over me. Christ, with his arms nailed to the cross, blood dripping down his face from the crown of thorns, now covered me in a crimson suffused with emerald and cerulean blue.

I'd like to say I was enraptured by the sacrifice, the resurrection, and all the Gospels had to share in the New Testament.

I'd like to say I felt the words penned in Paul's thirteen epistles.

I'd like to say I experienced the visceral presence of God, shared by a century of Christians who prayed toward the same altar I now stood on.

I'd like to say I found God again on this journey north to finish my novel.

I'd like to say that Megs had a hand in it, too; a modern-day disciple who found strays like me and lead us home.

But I couldn't say any of that. What I felt instead was something through the light and beyond the colors of glass.

What that was, however, was beyond me.

I felt it though; I even heard it in the tinny sounds of swing-set chains brushing against the old, hollow poles rusting from hot summers and harsh winters.

I felt all of it, yes. Through sound and sight and color and light.

I just didn't know *what* I was feeling.

"A lot of people do that," Starr whispered, almost reverently. "This place just affects you."

He caught himself, as if trying to take back what he had just said. "Well, it affects people like you. Like me."

I bowed my head, nearly in a prayer of thanks, then turned to face Starr, silhouetted at the entrance of the church.

"It's yours as long as you are writing. Should we walk over and let Megs know?"

I nodded, never even bothering to look at the converted sacristy or the kitchen.

"I think she already knows," I said, "but let's tell her anyway. I need to know what brandy to buy for tonight."

That was two months ago. In that time, Fear found me in new ways and held me in its grip despite Megs and Starr and the converted church. What started out as a barely perceptible chill evolved into a cycle of fevers that spiked almost daily. I had written next to nothing.

I didn't stop shaking from fever or fear until the early January storm ripped through Sherborn in the dead of night and the old oaks finally surrendered. The branch that shattered the disciples was followed almost immediately by another one splintering Christ.

I stand helpless at the altar, showered in glass shards, unable to move, and suddenly cold from the unexpected rush of winter all around me.

"*Jesus,*" I whisper.

Something changes in that breath, though. What I felt when I first stood on the altar two months ago returns.

Only this time, the feeling stays with me, and I begin to understand.

LEAD

When I chose to wake up an hour earlier this morning to write, I did not know what I would discover. All I knew was that I was accepting an invitation to enter a space where everything was possible. I discovered truths and energies waiting for me, desperate and patient, to be accepted, absorbed, embraced.

Sometimes, we just need to show up. What awaits in our space, and beyond, will take care of itself.

+++

In 1979, during a visit to my oldest brother who lived just a few miles away, I made the very bold decision to show him my sketch book. Warren was a talented artist who had devoted most of his life to crafting, painting, sketching, and creating just about anything his limitless imagination could conjure.

As he flipped through the pages of half-done sketches of strangers, a few landscapes of the woods around our cabin, and even some watercolor day lilies and wildflowers, he stopped at one page filled with triangular shapes of color.

"I'm fascinated with stained-glass," I said. "I know the combination of colors doesn't really make anything like a picture of a person or Jesus, but I love drawing these for how beautifully abstract they can be."

Warren, the consummate teacher and big brother, looked closely at my work.

"There's no space between the colors, between the pieces of glass," he said.

He was right. Nothing separated the colors but a pencil-thin outline I had used to make the shapes.

He went to his expansive library and pulled an illustrated art book from one of the top shelves. The scent of a centuries-old athaeneum slipped from the space of the heavy tome. Warren flipped through the pages as the musty dust filled the space.

"Look here," he said, stopping abruptly and pointing to an image of the Resurrection Cemetery Mausoleum in Justice, Illinois. The stained-glass wall stands floor to ceiling; an awe-inspiring work capturing everything from the crucifixion of Christ to modern-day inventions like satellites and airplanes.

"I never knew you could mix Christ with the trains that run through Chicago," I said.

Warren laughed, apparently aware of much more than I had known in my early teens.

"I'm showing you this picture not because of the images or even the glass," he said. "I'm showing you the space between the colors." He held my sketch pad next to the wall of stained-glass in the book.

"See the difference? You need space. Space separates the colors that comprise the bigger picture."

I did see it. Immediately. And in the years that followed, in the years I grew up, matured, and found my own path in art that distinguished me from my brother, up until his death in 2015 and now beyond, I see the defining lines of space that hold all of this together. You. Me. Us. The Universe. The Past. Today. Tomorrow.

The lines of space that cycle from piece to piece, from the floor to the ceiling, from stone archway to cemetery, from the heart to the mind to the universe. Love uncontained. Time undefined. Spiraling; circuitous cycles of unadulterated light, ever-present radiance beyond the boundaries of life filtered through self-defined suppressions and resignations.

"You need to make space to appreciate the whole. To see all that lies around us," he offered, closing the book and returning my journal. "Sometimes, it's what's not there that is most important."

✦ ✦ ✦

Each birthday, Warren bought me a new book. One year, it was *The Hobbit*, by J.R.R. Tolkien. Another year, it was *Watership Down*, by Richard Adams. We read them together. Discussed the journeys. Explored the imaginative worlds that, when we got right down to it, were similar to ours. Mountains, streams, warrens, even caves and holes in the ground.

We didn't do it intentionally. We didn't plan any book clubs or time to talk about the words; we just breathed the same story, found peace in the adventure, embraced the hues of cerulean skies and Kelly-green meadows. The creeks we wandered, in and out of the books, were as clear as the fluidity of forming glass, capturing light and life as it wound its way around the bend, on and on, into new worlds we could not wait to discover.

Maybe I also value "space" and seek it out as much as I do because it is what I grew up with. Not indoors, but behind our house, where a thin, trickling stream separated our large backyard from the spacious, magical woods. There, we built tiger traps and bike ramps of dirt and discarded tree branches, spied on Ol' Man Emil's broken-down house looking for ghosts and other apparitions just beyond the dirty, cracked windows, and crouched among thorny bushes waiting for somebody to pass us, and nobody to notice us. We had space to create, fight, play, imagine, grow and become independent. We were granted space, and our childhoods expanded to encompass all of it. We made it our own.

Warren and I took many walks in my late teens. Many of them were in silence, with just the muted sounds of the earth thumping through the walking sticks he had made. Other times he was Socrates himself, asking questions about the woods around us, the meaning of life, what mattered most to me in this world. The pauses between words stretched in our long strides around the water, along the ridge, and to the summit of our climb.

Sometimes, it wasn't the point to say anything.

The answers were in the space that surrounded us.

How do you find words for what is felt so deeply within you when you are a part of something so magnificent?

✦ ✦ ✦

Thoreau's words: "Simplify! Simplify! Simplify!" and Wordsworth's "The World Is Too Much With Us" were penned generations before the world of digital immediacy consumed us. They are lessons from a pre-technology world that are perhaps more relevant and urgent to us today than they were centuries ago.

✦ ✦ ✦

It was late September, 1991, when my college friend Bryan reached out to spend a day with me on the Chesapeake. Susan still had her boat in the water, and she invited both of us to sail on the Bay that afternoon. Susan was a teacher at our school, but she was south of where I lived in Calvert County and had some property on the bay's edge. I think she sailed every chance she had when she wasn't in the classroom.

Bryan was going through tough times. He was a philosophic soul in his early twenties, trying to break out of the box society kept placing him in. He showed up that day desperate for some space to sort it all out.

I listened, and Susan's boat on the Bay provided Bryan all the space he needed to find answers. It was on the water he decided to head to Greece, to live closer to the earth and further from the mainstream world. I witnessed the wind rip away his worry, his shrouds that bore the expectations of others, the demands he put upon himself to be somebody he was not.

When we returned to the dock at Susan's shore, Bryan – in all his shameless glory – had stripped away the heavy robes he once wore and revealed a larger-than-life, newly bronzed body that glistened under the late sun.

I never again saw the Bryan who boarded Susan's boat early that afternoon. Out on the bay, in the space it offered, he found the origins of his essence, and has held tightly to it ever since.

✦ ✦ ✦

A year after Warren died in 2015, I received a letter in the mail that he had left his entire library to me. My sister-in-law had boxed up most of the books by the time I got there to pick them up. Still on the shelves, however, as if waiting for me, were his copies of *The Hobbit* and *Watership Down*. I pulled them down with the care of a curator handling relics. The scent of musty dust met and enveloped me once more.

In his library, this sacred and ethereal space, I was with him again, carrying the words and journeys—the lives and adventures—we treasured along real and imagined paths. Where moments were not pushed but preserved in their immediacy. In the present.

I used to think *Carpe Diem* was all about being selfish, stealing moments, doing whatever you pleased, with reckless abandon. Now, it means seizing the stillness of the day's beauty as only you can. It took decades for me to learn this, however I wouldn't change a thing about how the definition evolved within me.

There is great growth in our failings, our misinterpretations, our blunders. Because of the desperation of my younger years, I am now able to value the ifs, whens, and possibilities around me with no expectations. The space provides.

Always.

ORANGE

One of the reasons I love revisiting my childhood public library in Loch Raven is the walk through the woods and across the long bridge. As a kid, I would often stop at the mid-way point where the brook runs under the bridge about 30 feet down. I'd stare at the soft stream of water, rambling over the smoothed stones, searching for fish to feed. I would pull out a crust of bread, stowed away in my coat pocket, and feed the fish I never saw. It offered a therapeutic practice; a taming of my teen-mind frequently overwhelmed and scrambled with the emotions and lessons of growing up.

So, when I began my long walk across the bridge yesterday to pick up a few mysteries I had reserved, I saw a young teen girl peering over the edge of the bridge, just about the same spot I used to stare at the stream.

As I approached her, she pulled pieces of something from her hand and let them take the long fall to the water.

How timeless, I thought. I instantly imagined another teen, in forty years, leaning over that same metal railing, feeding fish many generations removed from today's.

As I reached her, she brushed her hands and turned to walk

the rest of the way with me to the library. As we approached the front door, she stepped ahead, opened the door, and held it for me. I looked in her brown eyes for the first time and smiled, thanking her.

When she caught my eyes, I saw tears in hers as she fought for an outward show of courage. I walked in, held the second door for her, and noticed the unzipped Dora the Explorer backpack sagging off her shoulders. It had clearly seen better days, yet it had a certain Velveteen Rabbit wear to it, as if almost inseparable from her and worn out of deep love.

In this one-room library, there's no place to hide; a mere closet in comparison with the other libraries throughout the county. We crossed paths a few times and I noticed her tears had dried. She carried young adult mysteries and I imagined them pulled from the shelves with purpose.

When I went to check out my own three books—two mysteries by Ellery Adams and the latest suspense thriller by Dean Koontz—I looked for the girl. Before I left I wanted to check if she was okay, but she had disappeared.

I exited through the security doors and as I began to cross the bridge I saw her distinct pink backpack bobbing on the other side, heading toward the main intersection of Loch Raven and Taylor. I reached the mid-way point of the bridge and peeked over the railing, searching for the fish that were never there. After all, maybe the bread crumbs my friend had tossed would bring them out of hiding.

When I looked down, I didn't see any fish, of course. I didn't see any bread crumbs either.

What I did see frightened me greatly.

Ripped handwritten pages clung to the leaves of the trees weighed down toward the water, where a partially submerged stuffed bear clogged the slow flow of the stream. It was face-up, its little arms outstretched, as if hoping for a lift out of the cold water.

I turned back to see if the girl had turned around, possibly giving me one more chance to call out to her and make sure she was okay.

It was too late. She was gone.

I returned to the library, retracing my own childhood steps, reminded that cycles of pain and challenges never really end.

I stood there for a long time, looking into the woods, listening to the low rumble of the water tumbling over the rocks. I wondered if the bridge called to those in need, soothing us a bit, allowing us the chance to ponder our lives, consider our connections, and align with ourselves – and all that matters – to the most important beliefs we hold.

As I crossed the bridge a final time, I considered the significance of each step propelling me forward. As much as we might think we are moving ahead, we have to come to grips with the truth that there is no linear approach to living. It is recursive; an unavoidable circuitous trip. Eventually, we spiral back to the people, places and experiences that influenced us in our youth, and have an even greater impact on us as adults.

RED

I do not understand fear, how it works, when, or even why. I just know it gets in you, like some kind of perverse beast that feasts on you from the inside out. Slowly and methodically, chewing away at your heart and senses until your defenses are eroded like leaves devoured by the mandibles of microbial monsters. I have seen fear destroy individuals, right to the brink of death.

And for some, beyond.

For exactly 41 years, I have owned an acoustic guitar that has, for nearly all of those 41 years, remained dormant in its case, in the corner of my bedroom. The layers of dust resting on the instrument's hard shell are physical reminders of the fear I have of playing the harmless, six-string construction, lying neglected within.

There is nothing scary about it. My fingers would not bleed if I played, and the notes made by the purple marble pick pinched between my thumb and finger would be the same for me as they would you, or anyone else.

But for some reason, over those 41 years, I have convinced myself I am not a musician, nor a singer, despite decades of trying to be one, the other, or both. I'm not okay with this, yet I keep finding reasons to stay caught here, where I can't just push through and practice hard enough to get free of this riptide of fear.

Recognizing fear, I am told (and I preach to my friends who are giving writing a go), is more than half the battle. Look it in the metaphoric eye and it diminishes. Loses its hold. Falters enough for you to find the courage to take that risk.

If that is true, where is my courage? Even as I write this, there is solace in expressing a fear I am in no way tackling. I do not have my guitar on my knee, my left fingers in a C-chord position, or my right fingers poised to downstroke through the open notes EADGBE.

There's no PTSD here. I was not traumatized by an angry guitarist in my youth, nor did I have my knuckles cracked with a ruler every time I fell flat (or sharp) with a note.

So, if it isn't the instrument, and if I was not musically abused in youth, what is the origin of this fear?

✦ ✦ ✦

The first time I put a music CD in my car, I could not believe the difference in sound quality. It was so crisp, so digitally perfect, and so wrong. I will never forget the era of the cassette mixtape, traveling with me like a lover to New England, Ocean City, and everywhere else I went. We spent summers in concerts together along those American roads. The sound quality was perfect for blaring as we became duet-singing partners on the rise and fall of the mountains in Western Maryland, the smooth flats of the ocean dunes, and the rural roads of sleepy New England towns. Elton John, CSNY, The Eagles, and so many more jammed on 31-minute sides of magnetic-coated, polyester plastic film turning in rhythm to the rolling roads we journeyed.

I long for their scratchy serenades.

If I can appreciate the notes, the very sounds comprising music that soothes, that brings a calming stillness, a transcending experience – especially when not acoustically perfect – then why can't I align more deeply, more personally, and surrender into the notes I imperfectly pluck on the six strings of an old wooden guitar?

I am not afraid to write anything.

Poetry, short fiction, novels, essays, plays all make their way to me and out of me.

I may not always write with ease, or with grace, but I am never afraid to trust the process. Or what I will learn each time I sit to write.

Am I more able to bare my soul to you as a scribe than as a strummer of strings?

What could you possibly learn about me in the notes I play compared to the words I write?

That I am a coward; a roar full of fear, signifying nothing.

✦ ✦ ✦

Despite this, I will preach to my last breath that creativity was never meant to be some kind of end game, where we create solely to share with the world what our imaginations have spun.

No. The spark is, and will always be, what's most important. It ignites unique imaginative and innovative thinking and action.

What *you* imagine? And what *you* create? Both are something only you can bring forth.

What we have lost is the knowing, the trust, that the act of bringing something forth will always be, in and of itself, enough.

You are *enough*.

✦ ✦ ✦

Find what calms the mind, and do it often. For me, this is coloring Mandalas and Tessellations. Color between lead lines. Bold. Defined. Inviting.

More stories have been born, and more problems resolved, in the simple process of coloring in methodical, sometimes tedious patterns, where my mind takes a deep breath and exhales all the worry, the stress, the fear. Maybe I need to draw before I strum? Release those fears, and let the colors in the notes fill the air with music and courage and love.

It's just six little strings, right?

✦ ✦ ✦

James Taylor sings, "The secret o' life is enjoying the passage of time." It has been a personal mantra of mine since childhood, when I first heard it while camping at one of the parks within an hour of our home. The only electronic I had with me was a battery-operated cassette player. I absorbed that other White Album, JT's Greatest Hits, with lyrics in one hand and a pencil in the other to respool the tape when it got caught in the player.

It was the connection within the music that captured me: how the lyrics blended effortlessly with JT's soft plucks of guitar strings. And when the batteries no longer had the energy to spin the spools, to make the music play, I abandoned the sleeping machine to explore in the woods. Along the trails, music followed and stayed with me. Notes became shared melodies with the songs of robins and sparrows. The percussion of breeze-swept leaves fell like soft brushes on cymbals, and the beat of lapping waves against smoothed rocks was as if Max Roach himself were knee-deep and invisible on the ridges of the lake, sticks in hand, foot on bass, a whispered cool *yeah* carrying into the wind and back into the trees.

Why did I feel such a natural, melancholic bond with the solitudinal sounds of soft chords and raw vocals, mingling with the universe?

I was only 13, and yet I already understood, and embraced, the secret o' life. It was a reckoning with the earth, the spirit, the all of everything, where I was just a drop of water; I was just a single note in the symphony of life.

And here I sit, 43 years later, mired in worry and fear over finding my fingers across the steel strings of a simple instrument. Afraid of making a single note.

Yeah.

Oh. How many times have I yearned to return to that 13-year-old boy? To relearn all I have forgotten?

Maybe in order to grow, to evolve, we need to find and surrender to our own 2,732 degrees of transformational heat.

THE GLASS THAT HOLDS THE BRANDY

On that first night in November when I offered the bottle of brandy to Megs, she smiled in the amber light of the fire in the hearth.

"Wait here," she said, and lumbered through the door to retrieve two glasses.

Margaret "Megs" Sedgwick was not a young woman, nor was she neat, nor was she healthy. Her hair was a steel gray, tired in color and unkempt as it curled out and around her shoulders. It fell on a threadbare jumper dress made of brown corduroy, with a cream fleece turtleneck underneath. She wore wool socks that disappeared under the hem of the dress just below her knees; untied black boots that were now in fashion – though I was sure she had no knowledge or care of that fact – completed her outfit.

Before she left the room she smiled at me with crooked teeth and cheeks that held the shade of a dying rose. It was her eyes, though, an icy blue contrast to the fire's light that warned me there was more to Megs Sedgwick than I might think at first glance.

I eased myself into the comfort of the couch, enveloped

in the down-feather pillows all around me. The fireplace drew me in, and I lost myself staring too long into the flames. I was swept away in the recurring film reel of my father's last seconds: gasping for air in a hospital bed; running out of the metaphorical fire that had enveloped him for years as a firefighter. When he died, when that last brief wisp of air left him, I heard the wails of my mother, echoing out in the lobby as she ran toward me, arms outstretched, in utter disbelief of his death.

"That fire catches everyone," she said, louder than what felt comfortable in the room. I wondered how long she'd stood there trying to break my thrall. She offered a knobby tumbler. I took it, although I felt unsteady from the unexpected punch of memory.

She opened the brandy, poured too much in each of our glasses, and raised hers with a smile that glistened with the fire's gold light.

"Welcome," she said. "I'm glad Cathy found you."

"Cathy?" I asked.

"Oh, it's just what I call the old church. It's a good nickname for *Catholic*, don't ya think? Keeps the place a little more neutral."

I nodded, wondering what the original parishioners might think of the name.

"Some people get scared off from that word *Catholic*," she said, "even though they don't know of its origins."

Megs stared in to the fire and whispered, "*Universal*."

And then, with a little chuckle, she turned to me and we traded pleasantries until our glasses were empty. When she refilled them, I felt a warmth coursing through me that wasn't just from the fire or alcohol.

Megs let the brandy run freely, and when she settled her glass, I noticed half of the bottle was gone. "Let's get down to the real reason you're here," she said, her hair hanging over her left eye as she stared at me with the right. I could almost believe it had absorbed the amber from the fire, and now glowed hauntingly green.

"Well," I began. "I'm finishing this story I've been writing for some time, and I needed a place to –"

"Not why *you* think you are here," Megs cut me off. Her hand hovered over her glass but she didn't pick it up. I saw the way the uneven surface caught the light of the fire, reflecting shades of orange onto her skin.

"Let's talk about why *Cathy* brought you here."

STONE

I remember first her words, soft intimations of fanciful kings and lost little boys, as she read to me on the edge of my small, twin-sized bed. I would fight to stay awake, to learn the fate of the heroes she brought to life, but her voice was just too soothing to resist. Sleep would find me sooner than later, and my dreams were filled with their own happily-ever-afters.

I remember her last words: soft whispers of resignation as she lay dying in our childhood home, fourteen years ago this week. Now it was our time to sit on her bedside, sharing words of love and gratitude, letting her know it was okay to let go. Her job was done; we were all going to be okay.

Somewhere between the first and the last, my mother and I shared secrets without inhibition. We always had that sacred trust, and even in my darkest times, she was there for me with a patient ear and sound advice; without judgment.

She showed me what it means to live compassionately: how to find space and offer it to others in need.

The first book I remember reading, all by myself, was *Just Only John*. The story is of a boy who wants to be somebody else. He finds himself turning into a pig and an old man, among other things, until he finally is "just only John." From the very start, because of my mother and our shared love for books, I learned we cannot be anybody but ourselves. It is what we are best at doing. Nobody can do it any better than we can.

✦ ✦ ✦

When I was in fifth grade – on the verge of turning eleven – I challenged my friend's dad that love was the core of our existence. I used music as my argument's foundation, making the bold statement that every song ever written was a desperate cry to give, to mourn, to reclaim, or to receive love. I remember distinctly his laugh as he downplayed my case. In that laugh I also remember hearing something else: fear.

I didn't understand that fear then.

Forty-five years later, I do.

✦ ✦ ✦

For a multitude of reasons, too many people believe accepting and offering love is an inherent weakness. As if love replaces or negates a more robust strength of character or threatens to destroy a necessary facade that serves to deflect, to shield, to protect.

But from what? A loss, a broken heart, an unfulfilled promise, an unmet expectation, a dream unrealized?

What is so terrifying about letting the guard down? Of being vulnerable?

Embracing Love as a core element of our existence requires us to be both vulnerable *and* strong, empathetic *and* discerning, selfless *and* self-seeking, personal *and* universal.

But most of all, it requires us to understand that love is limitless.

Our decision to embrace it, to offer it – unconditionally – heals us and diminishes the grip fear has on us.

Love, in any form, is not conditional. It transcends religion, philosophy, science, race, ethnicity, gender and color.

I knew it when I was eleven, and I know it now: there's a reason why love permeates all things, from music to art to science to God to you and to me. It is the thread connecting us to our origins, our journeys, our destinations.

It is the thread tying us all together.

I loved you when I was eleven; I love you today.

Please, know that there is no either/or when it comes to love. There is love, AND there is everything else.

But first, always, there is love.

✦ ✦ ✦

Veronica was my first real "love" at the tender age of ten. One spring afternoon, we painted her treehouse an olive-green color. In the middle of paint-playing, she turned the wet brush to her hand, painted each finger, and then pressed her open hand on to my white shirt, covering my heart. It was the greatest moment of my young life. Five hours later, her friend called me, as I sat with my family eating spaghetti, to tell me Veronica didn't like me anymore. Trapped in the tinny odor of canned tomato sauce that suddenly nauseated me, I felt my heart break for the first time.

For months I kept that shirt tucked away in my dresser, only to pull it out each night and press my own hand against Veronica's olive-green imprint on my heart.

This was my first chance to become bitter and push love away. To close my heart, to not feel the pain or risk it in the future by being so open, so vulnerable.

Instead, I chose an even greater, universal love that I did not yet understand. Feeling pain made me feel compassion. It made me feel empathy toward others.

If I felt it so strongly, then surely others must too?

Every time I feel love today, wisps of tenderness run along the ridges of heart sorrows. Appreciating love in such a universal way could have never happened so intensely without feeling and holding the pangs of a broken heart.

Born out of heartbreak was a deeper love.

It infuses the olive-green stitches binding my heart with yours.

✦ ✦ ✦

I say "I Love You" with sincerity and ease to a level that is sometimes uncomfortable to others. It is born out of childhood goodbyes to my father when he left home to fight fires in Baltimore City. Some of his best friends never returned, killed in the Line of Duty.

"Good-bye" and "I Love You" really meant something.

Often, I'd be playing football in the street with my friends when Dad would leave for night shift, just about twenty minutes to four, four nights a week. He'd stand at his truck, waving goodbye, and I'd drop the ball I had just caught and run up to him, giving him a kiss on the cheek.

"Be safe," I would whisper. "I love you."

The night he died, I stood by his bed in the emergency room. watching a bone-shaped tube in his mouth help him breathe. I wasn't afraid to give him one last kiss on the cheek.

"I love you," I whispered.

✦ ✦ ✦

Love can never be diminished in the number of times we say it, express it, embrace it. Like a cherished but tattered toy, the love that makes it so cannot be undone or taken back; it's what makes all of this real.

In the words of Margery Williams, the author of *The Velveteen Rabbit*, "Once you are Real you can't become unreal again. It lasts for always."

✦ ✦ ✦

I can't wait to see what you want to show me, she says.

We walk hand in hand up the slope to my old school playground. When I was just seven and in second grade, I'd felt on top of the world in this land of pebbly, coarse sand and squeaky swings. I ran laps with other boys around the shiny, silver railings bordering the lot, unable to escape the clutches of the girls who caught us and dug their nails into our arms.

So this is it? This is what you wanted to show me?

At ten, we sat on those worn railings playing Truth or Dare with the girls. Truth was to tell – or swear to – mostly lies we wanted others to believe. We boys always believed each other; the girls were impressed by our storytelling style if nothing else.

Very nice.

When eleven, we jumped from the railings and ran across the baseball fields to hide behind the backstop and smoke our parents' menthol cigarettes and revel in just-discovered French kisses.

She wraps her arms around her chest, fingers holding the cuffs of her sweater tightly. Looking at the car, she rubs her shoulders: *I'm cold. I think I want to head back, if you don't mind.*

To her, this old playground under the early moonlight, this landmark of my innocence, is little more than a concrete pit filled with tired sand. She can't see how these coarse pebbles have absorbed countless falls, endless tears, numerous broken hearts and heart-quaking first kisses.

She stops, turns around. For a moment, I think she gets it.

Keys, please.

I toss her the car keys and turn back to the lime-lined field. I feel again the chain-link fence pressed against my back, digging in with each new kiss a girl pushes into me.

I'll see you in a minute, yes?

Lips on lips, menthol swirls, hands on backs, in hair, on necks.

Yes, I say, holding onto the space this playground holds.

✦ ✦ ✦

"The End" is the last song The Beatles recorded together. It was Paul's brainchild, and his line, "And in the end / The love you take / Is equal to the love you make," is probably one of the most powerful and simple mantras available to us.

✦ ✦ ✦

For a long time, I looked for the instant return and immediate gratification of reciprocal love. I was filled with expectations and desires that I demanded be filled; right now. When they were not, I turned bitter and thought Paul had it all wrong. I was too naive to see the bigger picture; too self-absorbed to get it.

It's a cumulative thing, this love we make and the love we eventually take. It's not a business transaction or some kind of back-alley deal we make just to get our fix of love. No one is meant to be keeping a tally. And especially not us. This isn't some kind of biblical eye-for-an-eye kind of pact. Love comes in many different shapes, colors, entities and beings that we must be open to receive, even in our darkest hours.

Sometimes, the love we eventually take doesn't even look like the love we originally made. It's a shape-shifter; a drifter from what we expected, desired, or hoped for. It's more than what we ever made though. We just don't recognize its different forms: a note from a student; the laughter of a child; the warm embrace of a stranger; the random phone call at 3 am "just because."

When it arrives – in whatever shape or color or form – sometimes we pass it along, choosing not to claim it, never realizing how great a gift it really was. That it was meant for us. Sometimes we realize it too late, because we don't immediately recognize it as the love we once made returning. The pain becomes a deep sorrow – unimaginable until we are in it – for what we lost of our own volition.

When we stop looking for what we expect – a mirror of what we made – we begin to see the boundless love offered every single day, disguised as the most beautifully simple and ordinary moments that matter more than anything we think we need or want. There is a magnificence in the mundane if we allow it. Love amplifies here.

This reciprocal, circuitous, limitless, unconditional thing called love is the universal energy at the core of all living beings. It not only connects us, it is us.

SAND

Too many stories are taken to the grave. I don't really know if it's because we think there will be more time, or if we think nobody really cares. Or maybe it's about vulnerability and what we're afraid it reveals of us. Maybe it's a bit of all three. The trouble in thinking about any one of these is it creates a whirlwind of ignorance, a false kind of stoicism, or maybe even an unintended selfishness. We cannot comprehend the depth or impact of our experiences and stories in the moment, so we take them with us even though they were meant to be shared. They were meant to be entrusted to others and left for the world to decide their merit in times yet imagined, unrealized.

This one has haunted me far too long.

✦ ✦ ✦

In June 1990, I spent a week on the Chester River (a Chesapeake tributary) with the Chesapeake Bay Foundation, along with ten other teachers. We started at its origin, a trickle of fresh water a few feet high on an otherwise non-descript hill, and followed it all the way down to its expansive spill into the Bay's brackish waters. On the fifth day of our journey, we arrived at a terrapin slaughterhouse just south of Rock Hall. The front of the worn building was hardly inviting, washed in variations of gray that had never seen better days. I don't recall it having a particularly appealing name. It was just a place to slaughter turtles, and some chose to stay outside.

I did not. I knew the Foundation wanted us to experience the darker aspects of the economy and ecology of the bay. As we studied our effects on submerged aquatic vegetation (SAVs) and rockfish, we had the chance to see a more direct impact on another species in the bay: the diamondback terrapin.

About half of the group entered the slaughterhouse, with our leaders, Don and Caroline, where we immediately stood in the dark antechamber that served as some kind of facade to the death rooms on the other side. After a brief introduction of the business of slaughtering and selling terrapins to China and other countries, we were led through a stained door into an even darker space.

The slaughter room was cold, and an acrid smell of fresh blood and stale feces and flesh washed over us, clinging to our clothes like a dirty stain.

We were first introduced to the filthy pens where the large terrapins were kept for days, sometimes weeks. Most were here legally, dredged from the bottom of the bay; others, though, as we later learned, were brought illegally by the thousands from other states along the mid-Atlantic and sold to be slaughtered and shipped overseas.

We moved to the next room, which was both colder and darker. A man straddled the shell of a large, live turtle. In his right hand he held an axe.

"I'm here to show you how it's done," he said. His voice was as rough as his appearance; there was an absence of any color in his clothes or his face. He was a moving, talking extension of the death energy around us.

"They like to hide their heads, as if they know what's going on." He laughed. "So we gotta encourage them to play a little peek-a-boo with us."

He raised the blunt end of the axe and smacked the turtle's beak peeking out from the safety of the shell's outer edge.

As soon as the turtle reflexively extended its head out of the shell, the executioner flipped the axe in his hand, offered a haughty "PEEK A BOO," and brought the sharp end down on its neck as hard as he could.

The blade cut through most of the thick muscle, but the head still twitched.

"Stubborn creatures," he mumbled as he raised the axe again. "We pride ourselves on getting them with one swing, but most of the time it takes two to finish the job."

He brought the axe down again. The head flopped to the right, attached by a thin tendril.

"And that's how you kill a turtle. Questions?"

One of my colleagues left abruptly to vomit; the rest of us stood there, speechless.

For the rest of the afternoon, we did our best to let the brackish winds rid us of the stench of death that clung to us, but nothing could cleanse us of what we wore, nor what we saw, that afternoon in the slaughterhouse.

✦ ✦ ✦

A few months later, when the moratorium on catching rockfish was lifted, some of us met up with Caroline and Don. We caught ourselves two 25-pounders and cooked steak-cut filets over the fire on the sandspit where we planned to spend the night.

When the fire began to die down, Caroline and Don buried the embers in the sand, and the rest of us searched for softer spots along the spit to sleep. We spread out along the stretch, throwing down our sleeping bags and makeshift pillows, and lay serenaded by the late-night song of a passing gull or laughing tern. The silence of man in the natural world gives space to a symphony of calls and splashes that plays on, with or without us.

We awoke before sunrise and immediately ventured out to the center of the bay beyond the four-mile bridge connecting the western and eastern shores. The rising of the sun, breaking the water's horizon, left us speechless. Despite the horrors of slaughter months before, the unexpected deaths of loved ones that had happened since, and the never-ending battles to protect the Bay's flora and fauna, the sun continued to rise. With the beginning of each new day, we were given the chance to see and experience the endless cycle of love and life in different ways.

When we regrouped, our minds were already focused on how we could get our students to embrace such passion for the bay and its future. We hadn't noticed that Don and Caroline had gone ahead of us to the spit until we stepped out of our canoes from the anchored boat. As we approached them, they held up their hands, stopping us in mid-step.

"Freeze. Look around. Something pretty miraculous is taking place," said Don.

For the first time, we were looking at the sand spit in daylight.

It was a little longer, and wider, than I had imagined. The previous night, I felt like the waves were closing in around us, especially with the rising tide. As we looked at it now, though, we were never in danger of being touched by the brackish waters.

"It's beautiful," one of my colleagues said. "But I'm not sure what is miraculously different."

Don took a few steps back and walked to our left; Caroline smiled and said, simply, "Look down."

We looked at the sands around us. One by one, we realized that the miracle was everywhere.

Tiny terrapin trails streamed from hatchling nests, terminating at the water's edge. Some made it to the lapping tide; many ended between the nest and the water, a tragic conglomeration of immature flippers and the frantic swoop of hungry seagulls.

"This, right here, is the life, and the death, and the life of Chesapeake Bay," said Caroline. "While we were snuggled in our sleeping bags, buried beneath us in their nests were unhatched turtles getting ready to break free and make the frantic dash to the water."

I thought about their struggles to survive in the first few moments of their life, and how we so mercilessly slaughtered them for money at the other end of their journey. I tussled with how much we enjoyed fishing for the rockfish the night before. How we sacrificed them for our personal feast and then talked for hours afterward about the joy of eating a fresh catch from the bay.

Where did I fit in all of this? The slaughter, the sacrifice, and the natural selection of who lives and who dies?

Don called us over to where he was crouched in the sand, staring intently at the ground. He was maybe fifteen feet from the water's edge. We gathered around and saw a single turtle fighting to make it to the water, hurrying as fast as his tiny flippers would carry him.

"Why don't you just pick him up and throw him in?" I asked.

Don shook his head, but smiled. "We are already infringing too much as it is. He needs to make it on his own. At least we can be a witness to it."

We watched the little turtle digging in despite the sudden crowd around him. We cheered him on as he inched closer to the shoreline, where his next round of instincts would kick in and carry him to deeper waters.

I stepped away, dumbfounded by the irony of the last 24 hours.

Our intrusions into the natural world are inevitable, if not fully hypocritical. On some level, we can't avoid advocating for the preservation of the bay and its wildlife while, on an entirely different level, we contribute to its destruction as we overharvest fish, crabs, turtles, or oysters for our selfish and capitalistic desires. We even push knives into the tops of our state fish in some kind of mercy killing.

Yet, in the mere passing of a single sunrise, we could rally around a lone baby terrapin and watch it make it to safer waters that, just as ironically, immediately presented a new round of dangers.

It only took a few minutes for the hatchling to make it to the water where his flippers, like little propellers, carried him away. We all stood and stared at his new home as a solitary heron flew just barely above the water's calm surface, searching for an early-morning snack over the path of our little swimmer.

The cycle never stops, I thought.

And we are a part of that cycle. Our lives, our stories, our journeys contribute to the miraculous Ferris-wheel spin as we merry-go-round the sun.

✦ ✦ ✦

That following Spring, Will (one of our school's science teachers) joined me in taking a group of students to six acres of marsh land on Broomes Island. We mucked our way as delicately as possible through the two-acre stretch to the shore of the Patuxent. Will led the way, and we stepped in his tracks, careful to minimize our intrusion. Before reaching the clearing, we paused as Will disappeared just beyond the tree line.

CRASH — Whoosh, dub dub dub... CRASH — Whoosh, dub dub dub...

We crossed the barrier with caution and joined Will, hunched down at the water's edge.

CRASH — Whoosh, dub dub dub...

Harsh, hungry surf ripped into the deeply rooted banks of big cordgrass, seaside goldenrod, and switchgrass. As each wave crashed upon the stubborn shore, it sifted back through the thick strands of grass, popping pockets of air before the next wave came crashing forth. Will watched the waves beat against the grasses just ten inches from his boots. I turned to look at our students, remembering something I had learned on the Chester River that summer.

"Who do you think's going to win?" I asked.

They offered a puzzled shrug.

"Between the grasses and the water. Who will win?"

One student walked to Will's side, and he stopped her with an outstretched hand.

"No need to handicap the grasses," Will said. "They've got enough to handle without the SAVs."

"The what?" she asked.

I explained that the fragile state of submerged aquatic vegetation had wavered over the years, mostly owing to the fluctuation of freshwater runoff into the Bay's tributaries and how, when SAVs thinned out, the waves got a stronger bite into the muddy shores of the marshes.

CRASH — Whoosh, dub dub dub...

Cautiously, she knelt down next to Will and watched in wonder as the struggle raged on. With each crash, another clump of big cordgrass loosened. The banks were already lined with gnawed-out notches. It was just one of so many natural-fought battles in the Bay's life cycle.

"The cycle never stops," she sighed.

Will looked up at her as if he was going to laugh, but he didn't. He squinted in the sun, and I never really knew if he was smiling or just reacting to bright light.

"You're right about that," he said. "And we're all a part of it."

ASH

As human beings, what do we carry? We live our lives as best as we can, but along the way we make mistakes, we run in fear, we grapple with the death of loved ones, and sometimes, in the process, we hurt others and that is a burden we have to carry.

Sometimes we even carry their deaths.

I have heavy, heavy boots for this one, every single day.

I left one of my teaching assignments early in the school year and headed north to Sherborn to sort things out. It was on the heels of my father's death, and I thought it would be the right thing to do – to leave that world behind and find some space to know myself again. I was selfish, making too much room for me while shutting hundreds of others out. I hurt some directly. I hurt others, too, in indirect and unimaginable ways. Of these, I learned through letters in the following months and years.

One hurts more than nearly all of the others, though.

Eric was in his very early teens when I had the honor to teach him. He was bright and inquisitive, but picked on by some of the other boys. Eric often stayed after class to chat about what we were learning. Our talks nearly always segued into something deeper, even philosophic at times, about growing up, the meaning of life, and, well, how to be Just Only Eric.

When our conversations ended, he would take a few steps toward the door, turn around, and blow his nose in the old rag he kept in his pocket.

"Thank you," he would say, wiping his nose one more time before leaving.

He always had a runny nose, and he always said thank you after we talked.

The thank-yous .... I always appreciated that about him.

He didn't seem so alone afterwards.

He was genuine through and through, despite what others did to, or said about, him. He was growing up, and I was witness to what most never saw in Eric.

So, when I took the leave of absence, Eric was devastated. I received this handwritten letter from him, and I wrote back almost immediately, but I never heard from, or about, him again.

Ten years later, a friend sent me his obituary.

Eric died of a heroin overdose.

Alone.

Aringinal time date and place
Time 9:36 night/bed room/11/17/92
Dear Mr. VW,

For the last month and few days, I have been a different person. I have sukseded in making enemies of Mr. E– and Ms. S–, and the end of the year is not hear yet. By that time I probably won't be asked back to the school. I don't want this to go on anymore. My grades have been going down and so has my self-esteem.

To get right to the point, you are the only one in my entire life time who has ever believe in me. And in a life I know, when that very spesial person loves and leves and know one believes in you, well I crie real sad.

The other day I started going off on Mr. E– because I had just had enough. I had a long talk with Mrs. B– about you. And I want you to know without enspireing these kids and me with your likeness I don't know what's going to happen. I have now one to talk to know without you.

You have been so much to me and my hole life. Every one wants me to change. Should I? I need your input. Is my life good the way it is, or should I become a now body just some one hews the same as every one else?

I ges what I'm trying to get at is that you just have to come back. I know this sounds corny, but I can't grow with know self estem, and I can't have self estem without you.

Mr. VW you are some one special in my life and I want it to stay that way. You have to come back. "You mean so much to me."

I rote this poem a few years ago knowing it mite come in handy at some time in my life. So hear. I rote this for you.

If you understand the segnificants in this you know how much you mean to me.

Tear Drops
by Eric, 1990

Tear drops filled with
so much feeling. But
so small a thing
could have more feeling
than anything else.
They are nothing more
than water and salt.

Tear drops just like
rain drops falling out
of the sky. They're just
Two differences.

Tear drops are filled
with feeling. And
nothing more than
Water and salt.

The End.

THE GLASS THAT STARR CARRIES AWAY

Before the sun rose, Starr had paneled the broken windows and brought in a pellet stove to warm the great room. By then most of the glass was gone.

"Don't move! Don't step on a single piece of glass!" he had shouted earlier through tears, running into the church, after the blasphemous branches destroyed the centuries-old artistry.

He'd stood shaking, looking in from the edge of the crime, then covered his face, blocking out the scene where his mentors had just been brutally slain.

I did as I was told. I remained still and calm. The fever in me was subsiding, an annealing of sorts, probably from the cooler temperatures filling the great space.

What each of us experienced in that moment was clearly unique: a meteoric shift had just occurred in my world, while a devastating crash had just torn through his.

Starr lowered his hands, though his eyes stayed closed; he took a few deep breaths, and then whispered words I did not understand:

Sicut erat in principio, et nunc, et semper, et in saecula saeculorum.

He ended the prayer by making the sign of the cross, then opened his eyes. Something was different now, and Starr seemed aware of what he needed to do.

"Not that any of this was unexpected," he said in exhale, and certainly not to me. "I just didn't expect it to happen so soon." He held up the palm of his hand to me, indicating for me to stay in place, which I did. Even when he walked out the door and disappeared for several minutes, I dared not move.

In that time, I looked all around me at the jagged hues scattered on the floor. I could make out a piece of Christ's robe, an outstretched finger, the reverent eyes of a disciple, a sliver of a sun sliced by an ominous thin crimson cloud.

But they were more than literal shards of a larger work that had endured longer than I had been alive. In the way they had fallen, I saw images – unmistakable yet paradoxically abstract – of a life yet imagined at any time in my existence here on Earth; previously unseen, still strangely familiar. In this chromatic glow of death and resurrection, another world, another time emerged, where what had been embraced as sin became respected as part of the balance between light and dark.

I had been held back, suppressed by fear; made to believe I could not do *this*; I cannot be *that*.

The reasons I was here – fear, love, anger, grief – all came together in that moment of annealing, and I felt something new forming. Something inexplicably amorphous. Beyond any label or box created to confine and control, to identify and understand, to diminish and silence. My body twisted, my arms stretched outward, my chin rose as my feet found each other and lifted me from a singular point on the floor.

"Why are you standing like that?" asked Starr, when he re-entered the church. He was carrying a long, shallow wooden tray of forty or fifty compartments in one hand and a battery-powered lantern in the other. He wore thin latex gloves, as if preparing for surgery.

I stared blankly at him, then noticed my outstretched arms and how the toes of my left foot covered the right. I dropped my arms immediately but did not move my feet.

Starr began the process of picking up the glass, considering each piece, slowly and methodically in the lantern-light, before placing it in a compartment.

"Megs thinks this church summoned me for a reason," I said, somewhat embarrassed.

Starr kept his focus on the floor and the glass, barely whispering an, "Ayuh, she does."

"Not to get too weird about any of this, but does she say this to everyone who answers the ad?"

Starr laughed as he picked up an elongated shard of emerald green and rehoused it in the wooden tray.

"When I was a kid, my parents would take me into Natick for the Spring festival they have every year," he said, sorting through the glass on the floor around us. "They would have a lot of artsy booths, live music from local bands that toured the high school circuit during homecoming and prom seasons, and WSNK would always set up a makeshift radio station to broadcast live. They'd invite you to give them a shout out between songs. Really cool stuff, especially for those of us who were into everything from roots of rock to the latest alternative music."

His expression lightened. "They were great days, for sure."

I nodded, remembering a similar event in my hometown of Towson where several blocks were shut for the Towson Town Festival. College students always flocked to it for the beer garden behind the courthouse.

"Anyway," Starr continued, his fingers now moving intuitively between the colored fragments and the tray. "The radio station always gave out grab bags of promotional CDs they had received. Each bag was $5, and there would be at least eight or nine CDs inside. You never knew what you might get, but every bag held promise. After all, it was the music you were listening to whenever you tuned in. Everything from the lost tracks of Buddy Holly to the haunting guitar of Will Ackerman. Like I said. You just never knew."

Starr was now behind me, and I stepped forward into the area he had cleared to face him.

"Ackerman's one of my favorites out of Windham Hill," I offered. "One of the founders of the music production group himself."

Starr placed a piece of yellow glass in the tray and looked up at me.

"Founders. That's what Megs looks for every time she posts an ad. Some of you who respond are like good music, and others? Well, let's just say the music she's looking to hear is something only the founders can play, whether they know it or not."

I slid my foot across the floor and found a splinter of blue glass tucked between the planks of the hardwood floor. The blood from my toe ran along the ridge of this piece of the sky and left a trail of dark purple in its wake.

I winced from the pain; Starr smiled.

"Better not let Megs know you offered up a spot of your blood to commune with Cathy. She'll run with that for sure."

"Noted," I said, pinching my toe and offering the glass to Starr. "What does she think we are Founders of, exactly?"

Starr shook his head. "No, no. Not 'Founders' as in people who are the first to own something, like land or a new-age music company." He stood up and took the tiny shard from me. The wooden tray was now filled with segregated colors. He placed the blue splinter into a compartment with larger pieces.

"Then what else do Founders do?" I asked.

Starr turned the lantern off and walked by me, heading toward the stone archway that led to the steps outside, then turned around and looked at me, eye to eye, for the first time since he returned with the tray.

"It's not the outside that matters to them. It is the inside they're most interested in," he replied. "They search and find what's elusive to most. Maybe totally unknown. They see it inside themselves and then work out how to share it with the world."

Starr's shoulders relaxed. The tray in his hands tilted toward me and the sections of glass radiated in their own light, their own hue; a hurricane swirl of color caught in the frosty dawn light filtering through the door.

"Megs. She knows you see it. You are the Ackerman in this year's grab bag of tenants."

GREEN

Whenever I go to the beach, I am reminded how fascinated I am with origins. The ebb and flow of tides. Of matters of joy and despair. Of life and how it is born out of chaos and the ancient battles between Gaia and others. I have dared to call myself an aetiologist from time to time: a seeker of the beginning of all things. With the rolling of the waves washing over my feet, I remember where I come from, and that such clashes are necessary to sustain a balance – tense and fragile as that may be – in our respective journeys.

✦ ✦ ✦

Before I wanted to be a teacher, I wanted to follow – albeit loosely – in the footsteps of my father and brother, who both served in the fire department for practically their entire lives. It wasn't fire that interested me as much as investigation, and I decided after my junior year in high school I wanted to be the person who tried to figure out who committed the crimes. The only TV hero I had at the time was a coroner named Quincy who was the precursor to every CSI and SVU show decades later.

I started out with a visit to my counselor, who said I was sick and people didn't really do that for a living. Nevertheless, I was determined to pursue a medical track in my last year of high school.

What I didn't realize was I needed a signature from the science department chair to take microbiology.

The chair was Ms. Abbott, my sophomore biology year. And that was going to be a problem.

My lab partner for Ms. Abbott's biology class was Sharon. For some reason we decided to save a section of each dissection with the intention of reassembling them into some kind of FrankenMonster at the end of the year. Sharon and I found it hilarious. Ms. Abbott did not.

So, when it was time to get her signature to take microbio, she refused. I pleaded with her. I told her I had matured. She wouldn't hear any of it.

Between a guidance counselor who thought I was disturbed and a teacher who had somehow forgotten people do stupid things in high school but actually learn from them, I was doomed. I would never be the next-gen Quincy.

What I did have, however, were three teachers who saw my potential as a human being and gave me the space to be stupid and learn and grow and own all that I did.

That was the key.

✦ ✦ ✦

Jack Delaney and Mike DeVita pushed me to the brink while never losing faith in me. Since the first day they met me (and I met them), they believed in me: as writer, actor, and individual. If it weren't for them, I would not be doing the things I love today.

Jack was the first to put me on the stage; this was in primary school. But in the classroom, he taught me the process of writing horrible first drafts, focusing instead on the power of revision. In high school, Mike put me back on the stage. He also gave me the opportunity to write plays with a view to produce and share them with the world.

These two men were more than teachers and directors; they were genuine, passionate, and authentic human beings who gave me space to see myself as human too. To start to take up the necessary space within myself and then in the world beyond. Teachers, man. They do that to you (well, most of them). They believe in you. So you can believe in yourself.

✦ ✦ ✦

Third grade teachers have the worst job ever. They pull out that red pen and break the hearts of writers who thought their words were special, perfect, moving. Jane Gordon was different. Her infectious laugh and boundless energy gave us courage to get beyond the heartbreak of critical feedback.

When that same third-grade teacher became my friend, 45 years after those come-to-Jesus classroom moments, I found myself in the hands of a mentor, a gift of the wizarding world, and all-around God-send as I continued to try to figure everything out, despite all I'd already learned.

Jane Gordon, you are my Dumbledore, my Gandalf, my Glynda.

✦ ✦ ✦

Some of the best teachers I have are not from the teaching profession. They are the fellow high school alumni I wished I had spent more time with in my youth. Listening to their stories as an adult, I came to understand some of what they learned along the way, as we all wondered and wandered along criss-crossing paths, intersecting at various points across the decades.

Sandy is one of those people. She lives in Nanticoke, about fifty miles southeast (as the crow flies) from the sandspit I spent the night on, where the terrapins hatched. She lost her son and her father in recent years, and now shares images on social media of the essence of the Nanticoke River: the sunsets, the crabs and the egrets, even the wild grasses that grow along the pier where she casts her lines in the water for a daily catch. Her father, before he died, tended to the wildlife around their land, and he even spoke of how the geese and heron would return to his property to die.

One day, in early July, Sandy was walking among the grasses by the water, when she came across a dying baby white heron. She wept for its suffering, and sat down beside it and held on to it as it died in her arms. She then returned to her house, gathered a shovel and a large paver, and dug its grave, placing the paver over the overturned dirt to keep the foxes away. She whispered prayers in reverence for this death, and prayed for the heron's peace beyond this world.

Despite her own grief for the loss of her son and father, she cared for this small bird as if it were another of her children. She rose above her own grief to provide space and witness this heron's young life that, even in the wild, ended far too early.

The cycle never stops.

We just get better at flowing with it in its ever-swirling whirlwinds around the sun.

We are the cycle, whose winding tendrils anchor and connect the past to the present, the present to the future and the future back to the past.

✦ ✦ ✦

And some of the greatest lessons I learned were from grown-ups who I never wanted to become.

When I was a student teacher, at the tender age of 22, an old teacher, pushing a cart with ungraded papers piled high and sliding toward the edge, shook his head when he saw me: crisp, energetic, ready to teach.

"Talk to me when you get to be my age. You'll burn out like the rest of us do."

I stared at him and thought: *the day I look like you is the day I quit teaching.*

✦ ✦ ✦

Maybe that's why I will always remember the lessons taught to me at a young age by Antoine de Saint Exupery and his Little Prince, to see the elephant swallowed whole by the snake, and not some silly Bowler hat lying on the ground.

We must hold tightly to the things that make us creative, vibrant, electric, alive. I'm that old teacher's age now, and I push that cart like the world is on fire.

✦ ✦ ✦

In my 34th year of teaching, I talked with a student about the difficulties of holding classes in two different classrooms, moving back and forth for each class.

"Oh, yeah," the student recalled, putting a hand to his chin and chuckling. "I remember you pushing that cart like some happy old man. It was piled high with ungraded papers that kept falling off in the hallway as you were rushing to get to class before the bell rang. You didn't care. You just kept going."

✦ ✦ ✦

We are the gatekeepers of the origins – the overtures – of our lives. No one knows us better than we know ourselves. The wisdom that resides within us from a lifetime of experiences deserves a longer listen, a deeper patience, to understand and embrace the beauty in each step we take.

I have never believed more in our future than I do today. I have seen the infancy of what is to come, through my treasured students, and I drift into these golden years knowing we're all going to be okay; they are going to be okay; the world is going to be okay.

BLUE

When I was seventeen and still in high school, I met a little girl with cancer who changed my life. Meggie was only eight when she died, but her death touched me in a way that prepared me for the passing of students and other loved ones in the years that came after. If I had "gotten over" Meggie's death, maybe I would have discarded the memory of her, too. That would have been tragic.

You never get "over" anything.

Rather, you absorb it and consider what to do with what is now a part of you. I can't close a part of who I am today any more than I can turn away from present experiences determining who I might be ten years from now.

✦ ✦ ✦

Most of the people I'd like to get over are too much a part of me to let that happen anyway. I think about the people who changed my life forever, like a boy named Sammy who punched me in the face when I was twelve and broke my front tooth. I was furious. I was also scared to death. With blood dripping from my lips, I shouted at others to hold him before I struck back. Later, Sammy would tell me he felt like he had to get one punch in before I took my own swing.

I don't know why that made me feel better, but it did.

That afternoon, my father called the police to take a report and see if there was a case for assault. The officer opened his shiny silver clipboard case, took down my statement, and then asked us if we wanted to press charges.

I know I did. I looked at my father, though, and waited to see what he had to say.

"What do you think?" he asked the officer.

The officer put his head down and stared at the muted reflection in the cover of his clipboard.

"Well," he began. "Sammy comes from a tough family that's going through some tougher times. His brother's on death row for killing a bunch of people. I don't know if you want to get tied up with them over an assault charge right now."

My father agreed. The officer left with a nod and an apology that any of this had happened.

I was outraged once he was gone. I didn't want to hear the story justifying letting it be; I just felt the sting of no punishment for what Sammy did to me.

For years I carried that anger, fantasized striking back, getting even, and punching his teeth out too.

But then it just dissipated. It went away with the changes of seasons, the coming of children, and the busy ways of parenting.

✦ ✦ ✦

Until I got a phone call at school from my wife, that our oldest daughter, Holland, had been in a fight on the playground. The other child had punched her in the face. There was a lot of blood. Maybe a broken tooth.

I jumped in my car and headed to the school to pick her up. On the way there, news broke on the radio that the longest person on Maryland's death row had been executed.

It was Sammy's brother.

The cycle never stops.

✦ ✦ ✦

After that summer when Sammy punched me in the face, I spent a lot of time in junior and high school sticking up for the bullied. But I crossed that line a few times myself. Stones, glass houses, all that stuff. I've made amends with most of them. Those scars run deep though and I will never be able to undo those hurtful things no matter how many times I apologize.

I'm human; we're all human.

The pain still lingers, nonetheless, and I will carry that to the end.

Maybe Sammy was hit hard by somebody else, long before our one-round bout in the backyard of a friend's house. Maybe it is true that cycles never stop: those who got bullied bully back.

Did the people I bully pay it forward and bully someone else later in their lives?

Or did some of them break the cycle and live the power of compassion before they were compelled to live out their revenge by proxy, on someone who never saw the original right hook that landed squarely in the mouth?

✦ ✦ ✦

The people you think you hate have origin stories no different to your own. You don't really hate anyone; you hate the metaphorical coat they wear to hide the hurt, cover the scars, and keep them safe. But that coat is also an emotional straight jacket that keeps them from feeling compassion and self-love. I was too young to understand, much less listen to Sammy's story. But my ignorance did not erase the story or make it never happen; Sammy's story existed and happened and hurt just as mine did, in its own way, with Sammy and his family.

It's hard to remember sometimes that those who reject love so adamantly are the ones who need it most, not just from us, but from themselves. We might be able to offer it, but in the end, they need to accept it, embrace it and see it in themselves.

We are all broken in some way.

Isn't it better to see ourselves as fragile human beings who are broken together?

I saw Sammy at a school reunion a few years ago, and we shook hands and smiled. That was it. I don't think we really needed to say anything else to each other.

✦ ✦ ✦

Many of my closest friends today are from high school, yet surprisingly not the ones who were closest to me then. That saddens me. The lovely few people I spent every moment with in years 11 and 12, now say they have "grown out" of me.

Sometimes I mourn the loss of friendships like I mourn the passing of loved ones.

How can they "outgrow" me?

What did I do in my older, wiser years, to turn them away?

The ones with whom I am closest with today are genuine, sincere, authentic, life-embracing individuals I wish I had have spent more time with forty years ago.

I am sorry about that.

I am grateful for who is in my life now.

Together, we are growing older, and if not wiser, than simpler, together.

✦ ✦ ✦

There is as much illumination in a single flame as there is in a roaring bonfire. It isn't in the ferocity of the fire; it is in the oxygen of ages that we share around it, the bonds of friendship that weave tightly in the wisps of wind-blown smoke, the sudden glowing of embers in our collective sighs, the moments where we cannot distinguish gravity-defying sparks from newborn stars.

✦ ✦ ✦

We lit individual candles for the children and teachers killed at Sandy Hook Elementary School in 2012; I carry with me their names held in the soft flickers that blurred through our tears. The power of light, the offerings of love, the communion of souls in such ceremonies of connection will always remind me that what we hold in the deepest origins of who we are cannot be questioned. We are the very embodiment of love, and that love was always meant to be shared.

✦ ✦ ✦

The more artificial light you extinguish from Earth, the more natural light you see in the sky filled with nine thousand stars. I am forever amazed by this. It takes the deepest dark to reveal the bountiful pin-pricks of light, sewn wonderfully in a sky of black.

✦ ✦ ✦

And the sun always rises, no matter the clouds or darkness that might dim its light.

SAND, ASH, STONE, FIRE

1971

Wes, as my father was known in his firehouse on Greenmount and 31st Street in the heart of Baltimore, introduced me to fire when I was six. He was taking me to my first Orioles game and decided to park behind the station, just a few blocks from Memorial Stadium, home of the Baltimore Orioles. When he opened the back door to the firehouse, the acrid rush of diesel filled the air around me, *filled me*, as I stood before a magnificent and intimidating sign on the back of Truck 7.

He led me on a tour of the station, walked me up the black iron steps that spiraled tightly to the left, and offered me a chance to slide down the fire pole, which I declined. When we returned to street level, he lifted me with ease into the driver's seat of the hook and ladder. I stretched my arms around the steering wheel, peered over its edge to see the back of Engine 31 so close to me in the narrow station, then reached up to pull a blackened cord that rang the fire bell loudly.

That illusion of being a firefighter – being just like my

father, Wes – ended before I could realize what was happening.

A booming voice echoed in the fire hall, dispatching both fire engines to a service call. Wes grabbed me out of Truck 7 as firefighters jumped into fire pants and boots while the firehouse gates rolled up, revealing a bustling Greenmount Avenue. One firefighter ran out with flags and stopped traffic as Wes carried me to the side of the station.

Sirens wailed. Bells rang. Horns blared.

From my father's strong arms, I watched Engine 31 and Truck 7 rumble past us and out of the station.

I wanted to follow them; chase them out the door.

The front gate began rolling down just as Truck 7 cleared the house, and I looked over Wes's shoulder to watch that magnificent, intimidating sign turn left and out of sight:

BEWARE: KEEP BACK 500 FEET AT ALL TIMES.

22 APRIL 1989

Several hundred feet from where my father lies dying, I sit against painted concrete in a cold hallway at St. Joseph's Medical Center, watching the EKG monitor above me. Dad's life line is erratic, jumping from zig-zagging peaks to near-flat lines that make me think the end has finally come for him. He is taking his final breaths after a medic call in 1986 infected him with hepatitis: a prolonged, agonizing death, in the line of duty. With me in the hallway is my brother-in-law, Rob. We have spent the last thirty minutes in silence, just a fraction, though, of the seventeen hours since paramedics brought Dad here.

We are outside a small room where Mom sits with my sister and two of my brothers.

Dad remains on a gurney through double doors and down

another hall. My brother Jim, who fights fire in Baltimore County, is with him, as is our grandmother and a few other family members.

I keep my distance. I've already said goodbye.

My eyes return to the monitor, where the zig-zagged peaks have become frantic. I look to Rob, who has nothing but strength for me, and I rest my head against the cold concrete and close my eyes. Monotone whispers seep from Mom's room but have no meaning. We all pass this time a little differently.

What feels like only a minute passes.

I open my eyes and catch the monitor: the peaks are gone; subtle bumps melt away into a flat line, and then the screen goes black.

1999

That's when I learned about The Dungeon.

That year, when our oldest, Holland, was three years old, we attended the parents' meeting at Heritage Montessori School, located in the basement of a church in Perry Hall. They covered the essentials: curriculum, whole-child learning, and the Montessori philosophy. As parents, we were excited to have Holland be a part of such a nurturing, child-centered program for at least the next three years.

When the headmistress concluded her presentation, she paused. She bowed her head slightly and said, "We just need to talk about one more thing: The Dungeon."

We looked around to the other parents in the small room, puzzled.

"In light of the event that occurred at Columbine High School in April," she said, "we have devised a plan to keep our children safe in the unlikely event of an attack on our school."

My heart absolutely sunk. This is my sweet, innocent, three-year-old daughter. No one would ever attack her school. Would they?

The headmistress continued. "Our plan is to break up the children as much as possible to avoid any kind of mass attack on them as a group."

I gasped at this image, and I wasn't alone.

"So, each class has a different route to the place we call The Dungeon," she said, "which is the safest place here at the school for all of us."

I left the meeting rocked with emotion, realizing how close the horrific touch of violence could come to my precious child.

Throughout the year, they held drills. She was being trained to "scatter" to reach a place called The Dungeon before a person with a gun could reach her.

Later that same school year, a man by the name of Joseph Palczynski, Jr. terrorized the area for thirteen days, killing four before a Baltimore SWAT team pumped 27 bullets into him and freed three hostages. We all breathed a sigh of relief that the reign of terror was over. Bill Toohey, then the spokesperson for the Baltimore County Police Department, said we could all get on with our lives as normal and with no fear.

And he was right; we could, and we did, for a year or so.

Then 9/11 happened, and our vulnerability as a nation became horrifyingly clear.

Our lives changed forever, in our communities and throughout the country.

2002

Thirteen months after 9/11, in the last days of the terrifying three-week stretch in October when the Beltway Sniper terrorized the Maryland-Virginia region, the needle on my gas gauge dropped another notch toward "E." I knew I was just fumes away from the bright red "fill tank soon" warning: the do-or-die situation of either get gas now, or run dry and walk to get gas later. My choice, really. A year or two ago it would have been a no-brainer what to do.

And usually, it still was.

In the wake of the infamous day "we will never forget," when we were all hypervigilant in every action, every move, was I more or less naive to think I wouldn't be the next victim of the sniper terrorizing my community?

Holland was now six years old, and she had not played outside in three weeks. Her school continued to be in lockdown, a term she now referred to casually over dinner. I refused to take her to any of the area parks (most of them were gated shut anyway). Just like the gas stations, and just like the superstores, they were all located – for our convenience – just seconds from a beltway, an interstate, a highway.

Easy on–off access. Designed to make our lives convenient, efficient, normal.

Normal.

Forget any hope of living life "like normal," as we had been encouraged to do by local politicians and law enforcement officials.

There was no longer a fixed definition of *normal.*

Normal had become a fluid interpretation, constantly redefined every time a .223 hit its target: an innocent mother, son, grandfather still living by yesterday's definition of *normal.*

Normal had morphed into thinking like an undercover security agent wherever I went. A once-normal trip to get groceries meant my wife took the kids out of the van while I scanned the area, looking for prime hiding positions where a sniper might lie, waiting for a clean shot.

"*P.S.:*" the sniper wrote on one of his notes, "*Your children are not safe anywhere, at any time.*"

I now lived my life eliminating possibilities.

Here's the way I had to think: The store blocks the south, and the west is filled with brick buildings. To the east I see a small clearing between two businesses. Just past the clearing is a quiet road with a wooded area beyond. I have never noticed that patch of woods. But now, I do. By my estimate, there's maybe 150 yards between us.

We are right in his range, I think to myself, *and I can't see beyond the first line of trees.*

Normal was now thinking like a master chess player, planning three or four moves ahead. You mapped out the escape routes he might take, the easy access ramps he might use to slip onto highways. Then you reacted by packing people around you like pawns to take a hit before you found yourself in check. You wanted to be ahead of the game, smarter than your opponent, cheat fate.

Normal was now thinking like the executioner himself. You pictured yourself as a target, viewed through the scope, tracked, locked in. *Maybe I've already been tracked, you thought*, but the timing was just not right, or a traffic signal turned green earlier than expected. Maybe you were just part of the rehearsal before the real hit. Maybe.

The gas stations remained empty all day.

My gauge moved lower.

My wife worried and wanted to come with me to get gas. "Better in numbers," she said. But the kids will be with us, I thought, and I don't really want them to witness my execution, should that actually happen.

So, I let the gas needle fall closer to "E" and spent the extra time with my family.

Those days, I could not hold my children long enough.

2009

My children. *My children.*

In the abyss, where there is a total absence of light, how do we find our way?

In the crossing of the calendar year, the second of two former students die by suicide within months of each other. When I read the news, amidst RIPs in social streams where there is no comfort in a flat digital screen in my hand, I realize suddenly the world is draped in darkness. I turn off my phone, feel the dead weight in my hand, and look for light in an absence of color. All I see are monochromatic shades of ash burying emojis of sadness on the blank screen.

I fight back. I want others to find light when they believe there is no more color in their world. I attempt to help by creating an organization as a bridge to the resources in need, but friends I once counted on convince me my efforts are not needed; there is already too much of what I do in the world.

Why do I listen to them? Why do I let them build walls when I want to build bridges?

Who owns this fear on either side of these colourless blocks?

Stunned, I blink away the shadowy anger and seek answers in new light.

Years later, I push on anyway and make a video that shocks others into understanding. I speak of my own moments of being broken, confessing injustices against me in my youth. But I do it to break through the Teflon coat of so many guarded lives. Hours later, after the video airs, a student I don't know comes up to me after lunch and thanks me. A glint of prism light shines through his tears, and that's when I know. That's when I see light beyond the darkness.

Years pass and twenty children and six teachers are gunned down in an elementary school five states away. I find myself back in the darkness but my own students emerge and rally the world to make yellow-green bracelets in support.

Hand-woven light to color arms. A belief in transcending love.

Hope to lift up strangers.

Another suicide later that year in a sister school and the community we helped states away wants to reciprocate, yet my school system throws up the wall: blocks compassion, volleys back their colors of kindness.

It no longer matters. Students weave secret bracelets in blue. They go underground to bring light to those in the throes of their own abyss just miles away.

At all turns, the chasm persists, but we are obdurate in its work. We move through blocks we are meant to believe are impenetrable. We persevere. The silken threads of blue, yellow and green reach out to us, pull us through, and remind us of what is possible in the clearing.

We embrace the prismed lines of light emanating from the lives we touch. And we are held. We are given a chance to heal.

Sand. Ash. Stone. Fire.

Even when we do not believe it, light waits patiently for us to see, to receive.

To be.

2019

The Darkness returns.

It is late Friday, just after 10 p.m., and I turn off the news and walk toward the bright red bullseye on the front of the plain stone building. The news reverberates in my mind as I walk through the glass doors. A rush of cold air greets me; a sterilizing splash that neutralizes the world still spinning out there.

Virginia Beach, 11 dead, 6 injured, suspect dead.

My daughter reminds me why we are here, in Target, and we march along the silent aisles, just like I did on that clear night nearly 18 years ago.

Planes into buildings, thousands dead, suspects sought.

I feel embarrassed, out of place, a fool for going about my business picking up cream for tomorrow's morning coffee while families are being notified that their loved ones are dead; their lives will never be the same.

And yet, here I am, seeking normal, craving sterilizing silence, desperate for a task to keep me busy, occupied, distracted from what awaits outside those smooth sliding doors that seem so protective, comforting.

Isolating.

I continue shopping while the weeping of mayors seeps through my veins.

Cream. We have come here for cream.

I stand in a random aisle and listen to the swelling silence around me. There's a hint of a page over stereophonic walkies for customer assistance in aisle seven. It only adds to the dystopian nature of my time here, in the wake of tragedies that cry out for anything but the normal response.

Thoughts and prayers, more gun control, we demand action.

I remember a shot-less victim's voice on the news telling me through tears that all she thought about was getting home to her eleven-month-old baby.

The lives of too many change in the hours after such a tragedy.

And yet…

yet –

We say our prayers. We take to the streets. We demand change while the next suspect loads up another cartridge and sets his sights on the ones who made him feel this way.

I walk up to the cashier, a man half my age with the name tag "MR. BILL" helps me navigate the transaction. I am more flustered than I originally believed. But of course, I'm also looking out for pickpockets, thieves, and gun-slinging disgruntles.

It makes me want to know what the afterlife is really all about, if it is about anything at all.

I think about other-worlds. up there, with the victims gathered together for a purpose they hope we will hear. They are the wise ones, after all. A cloud of witnesses. The whispers of first graders gunned down, of college kids and grandmothers, of high school seniors, all part of a club clamoring for some kind of voice, some way to break through the stratospheres of chaos and insanity, to rain some wisdom down upon us.

My daughter tells me it's time to head home, and she leads the way through the sliding double doors.

The air out there is heavy, and yet…

yet –

I step through and slug through the night, heavy boots heading home to busy routines that mute the madness out here.

The next day I stay off the news, walk to the beach, sink into the sand, and fill my head with jazz blues and the sounds of Miles Davis. I allow the notes to resonate, to marinate within. A swirl of temporary healing until the next tragedy breaks through my feeds, trumpeting fear, madness, and the same heavy weight of helplessness that has me searching for the bullseye target of sterility to get me through.

In my Miles Davis-infused meditation, I slip into a dream of weightlessness, and I become the Catcher in the Sky, building an impossinble high rise to reach the victims. If I can't save them here on this gravity-soaked America, I can grab my hammer and nails and climb high, leave behind the memories of senseless deaths and join them in their common-place space; ask for admittance to the exclusive club they never wanted to join.

There I can apologize for our ineptness at dismantling this fixation with guns and violence and death.

How do we stop it? I ask, hammer still in hand, when I step out into their liminal space. *How do we mend fences and rest weapons in bottomless bins; send them beyond our earthly plane? How do we dissolve the membrane separating us and allow zero-gravity wisdom to reach us, teach us, save us?*

They smile resolutely, but offer no words. Instead, I feel their wish in the aether around me. I absorb their wisdom and close my eyes, desperately holding on to the wistful permeations all around – and in – me.

I understand. I nod as I feel myself pulled down, hammer first, through the barriers.

Down
    and down
        and down
            past the infinite floors of flimsy
            pine my high rise is built from
            past the lobby
            returning to the sandy ground.

Terra firma.

I turn toward my house and emerge with new wood and tools. My daughter joins me.

Maybe this will make a difference, she whispers.

I pull a thick black marker from my pocket and pick up a fresh piece of pine, two inches by ten inches by twenty-four inches. With quick precision, I pen the letters as big and as bold as I can. When finished, I pull six four-inch nails from my other pocket.

She centers the handmade sign atop the entrance, and I pound the six nails into the wood – bullseye strikes on each nail – securing the sign to the frame.

I step back, dwarfed by the Miles-high high-rise soaring into the sky. Open pine planks so skeletonesque, so transparent. Fragile and strong.

My eyes fall floor by imaginary floor: three, two, one, and settle on the black letters etched across the just-nailed plank.

HOPE

I smile, resolutely, and raise my hammer to the letters as my daughter raises her hand, effortlessly as if in zero gravity. We tap the sign as we walk through the entrance.

Passers-by stop. Read the sign, and approach.

There is hope, they think.

There is hope.

There is.

Hope.

In the tests, in the bold statements, in the tears and in the cycles we are reminded of the fragility of life.

Hold the stones and ash and sand to the fire and become glass. See beyond.

Hold the broken shards of color. Reflect prism-like beams.

Hold the fractured light. Focus it with love.

Light exists in and beyond all. A light filled with love,

filled with the memories and lives of the ones who have held us together along the way: that's what I keep close. That's what I see.

That's what we are.

Light and love.

Always.

✦ ✦ ✦

I had just entered my fourth decade of teaching at the time of the Virginia Beach massacre, but I discovered a new strength and encouragement to persevere from the tragedies of the last twenty years.

I came across the letter my sixth-grade teacher, Jack Delaney, wrote us in 1977 as we "graduated" from elementary school and moved on to junior high. It seemed as if he were reaching out to me, from my past and beyond the grave, to bring new light to my journey, now well into the 21st century.

Here's an extract of most of what he wrote:

Think About The Sun!

It has been said that time flies when you're having fun. If that is true, then you have allowed me too much fun. I don't really know why it is June when it should be October. You have given me a chance once again to appreciate the beauty of the human being. You have shown me that it is everyone's differences that allow life to be a wonderful sharing experience. I look back with tearful sentimentality on the sad, hysterical, pleasant, joyful, insane moments you gave to me and I hope I gave you at least one moment of the "reasons for living" that you gave me!

I imagine that many of you would expect me to talk about your lives in relationship to a musical. Ha! Ha! I will. You know where you are going but it is important that we always see ourselves when we get there. That can be a way of coping with the joys and the frustrations of growing up. Don't always worry about today, but live for today and tomorrow. Whether it be dating, football, art, music, drugs, parents, teachers, English, math, or the world – there will always be a tomorrow and I want you to feel good about you when that tomorrow arrives! My fifth all-time favorite musical, "Pippin," has a magnificent closing song that is most appropriate for you today and tomorrow. Pippin is a young man who doesn't know what he wants to do when he grows up. He only knows he wants to conquer the world and have everyone know him by name. His friends sing to him to realize that he must be happy no matter what he does, be it conquer the world or sell ice cream in Texas. I think that you must be happy with you no matter what you do or where you go.

Jack Delaney :)

And in the song that he quoted before signing off, the essence was this:

Happiness resides in your journey when you seek to find your corner of the sky.

✦ ✦ ✦

I was fortunate enough to see Jack in my first year of teaching before he died in 1988.

I wore a bowtie that day, in honor of the outrageous outfits he wore every day when he was my teacher at Pine Grove Elementary.

"Thank you, Mr. Delaney, for helping me find my corner of the sky," I said to him, as I shook his hand. "I hope to inspire children like you inspired me."

He smiled and straightened my tie. "Jesus, Rusty. Just be

yourself. You'll do fine."

I never saw him again.

So, Jesus, Jack Delaney, we're doing our best to be ourselves. Despite the tragedy of the new normal, despite deadly pandemics, despite endemic casual violence, we're trying.

After all: The sun always rises, no matter the clouds or darkness that might dim its light.

We need to continue to see our children and ourselves as beautiful individuals who have the potential to change the world. To be more robust containers for love and for light. For it's in each of us: to live as light; to live as love.

For today, and for tomorrow.

For always.

THE GLASS THAT CARRIES MEGS AWAY

After the storm, after I had dismissed all of Starr's silliness about Founders and grab bags, and in the darker space of the great room now that he had blocked the holes left by the shattered panes of glass, I resumed writing at a feverish pace, uncovering deeper plot lines and character origins than I ever realized were in me. The ideas flowed so powerfully and with purpose that I dared not stand in their way. I was a conduit, and I was in awe of where the novel was going. I could sense a new light within the story; a presence I had never known much less courted. My novel didn't fit any mainstream genre now; it was a collage of epiphanies coalescing to form something unexpected, defining itself as it emerged.

I was excited to share this breakthrough with Starr and Megs. I drove into Natick to get a better bottle of brandy – this time a bottle of eight-year Asbach – and headed over to Starr's studio to invite him over for a glass with Megs at the farmhouse.

When I entered the space, he was in the corner with the tall piece of dogwood leaned against the wall. I could hear the soft plucks of guitar strings from a small cassette player as he worked feverishly on a long pane of colored glass. On a separate, smaller

›oden tray filled with the shards from

‹e. He worked on without even a nod or

pushing out the word with more force, of Asbach in the air as I walked toward him. ıts to celebrate a breakthrough in my writing. I ›u and Megs might –"

d around slowly, and I noticed immediately his d, to the point of being bloodshot. I wasn't sure if ı the strain of focusing so hard on his work or a lack

‹egs is by the fire, staying warm," he said, his voice raspy. ‹I appreciate that bottle. Don't bother knocking. I'll be ‹t over."

I stopped and looked over Starr's shoulder to get a good ‹ook at the project he was working on. The shape of the pane was unmistakable.

"Starr, isn't that–?"

He shook his head to stop me.

Holding my eyes with his, he said, "Go now. I'll be over in a few minutes."

When I entered the small room, Megs lay curled up on the couch in front of the fire, wrapped in a heavy brown blanket. The curls of her steel-gray hair fell down along the curves in the blanket and touched her folded hands resting on her chest. When she saw me, she smiled. When she saw the Asbach, her eyes widened with a glint beyond the light of the dying fire in front of us.

"Starr will be right over," I said, almost reverently. "I wanted to celebrate some unexpected, rather epiphanic moments in my writing with the two of you."

I offered her a soft smile, putting down the bottle and adding another piece of gnarled wood to the fire.

"I'm finding things, Megs," I said, walking into the kitchen to get clean glasses. "I don't know how you or Cathy do it, but I've never written like this in my life."

Megs stared into the fire, maybe even through it, to something only she could see, like the first night I sat there. I poured brandy into our glasses and offered a toast to the Founders who had come and gone from Cathy's auspice.

Megs held on to the glass, but did not drink. Her gaze stayed steady on the fire, tears brimming.

"She's dying," said Starr, now standing behind me. "It's been coming for a while now. She wanted us all together."

Megs turned her eyes to Starr, a faint smile pushing her flushed cheeks as she tried to raise her glass.

Starr moved to the couch and brought the brandy to her lips. She took a sip and Starr wiped away a drop of Asbach from the corner of her mouth.

Megs turned to me.

"I don't need to tell you what you already know," she whispered, her tired voice the sound of sifting sand. "All I've ever wanted to do is provide a space for Founders, for people like you who need to get away from the boxes, the pre-ordained paths, the lineage of what our ancestors deemed right, natural, necessary. To absorb the prisms in love-stained light that most of us never even see, much less realize. We must understand that what lies within us, in front of us, and beyond us can exist mutually, even harmoniously. There is no one path. Each contributes to the cycles. Each of us is already rich, filled with what we wish to receive. We are all creatures seeking understanding. A never-ending, cyclical pattern that overlaps generation to generation, century to century. Who are we? Where do we come from? Where are we going?"

I looked at her and waited for her to go on, but I knew she was nearly gone.

"Fear seemed to always hold me back from looking beyond the obvious," I said. "To see the symbols but not understand their meaning. Too scared to ask why, let alone how."

I took a sip of the Asbach to warm my throat. "I've been lost on the long-ago constructed walkways, in the expectations, the heavy ways of conventions and carry-overs from what has always been the way of the masses. I looked but I did not see."

Megs closed her eyes and gave a long, heavy sigh. "We are all just trying to find the light within the prism that is right for who we are, but you are correct. It is hard to discern what lies beyond what the eyes have been trained to see. It's not found in any one place. It is all around us. In us. Beyond us. All the time."

Starr gave her another sip of brandy; Megs opened her eyes, and the amber light found them immediately.

She turned back to me, and I stepped up, next to Starr. I leaned in and placed my hand on hers as she spoke.

"Stay as long as you wish. Cathy has been looking for you for a long time. Starr will transform the broken glass into something new, I am sure. Maybe the two of you will figure out what that might be."

I nodded through my own tears.

"Good night," she offered, resting her other hand on mine and closing her eyes.

I left the bottle of Asbach on the table and let Megs and Starr have their time in the room with the dying light.

Megs died the next morning.

Four days later, we buried her in the cemetery behind the church. Starr and I took turns digging the grave. The sounds of the shovel hitting stones in the ground fell in harmony with the tintinnabulation of the swings on their old hollow poles, carried by the breeze.

When we lowered Megs into the ground – in a casket Starr made of old and new glass, swirled with celestial stars around a colorful, wind-wisped rosary – the haunting sounds of flute and guitar in Will Ackerman's "Wondering Again What's Behind The Eyes" played on the old cassette player leaning against the handmade headstone marker. The ancient piece of dogwood was adorned with the rosary, now hanging on the crossbar, made from a piece of cypress. It was decorated with colorful, embedded glass that read, simply, "Margaret Sedgwick."

When we had finished burying her and offering words and silence in the space we had made for her, we returned to the church. Starr poured the remaining brandy from the bottle of Asbach. We toasted to Founders and then removed the wood panels where the stained glass had been. From the window, where Jesus had been crucified on the colorful cross, Meg's grave, with her own cross, filled the open space.

"She was serious about you staying," said Starr. "I'm going to need some help here anyway as I work to replace these windows."

"I accept the offer," I replied, my eye catching a stray glass shard on the altar. "I'm sure you have plenty of pictures to recreate what was here."

Starr shook his head, eyes never leaving the cross marking Meg's final resting place.

"That's another reason why she wanted you to stay." He took a step closer to the open window.

"Do you remember that first day you arrived, and you walked up here to the altar and stared at that image of Christ on the cross? But you weren't looking *at* it. You were looking *through* it."

"Yes. I didn't understand then. I do now."

"I need you and what you now understand to help me create something new that Megs would want for Cathy."

"The stuff of Founders."

"Yes. As a young child, Megs saw it in the eyes of her classmates who sat among her on the pews in this space, even though they struggled to understand themselves. This church, this space…everything is bigger than any one of us, at any time in our existence. But that everything is also in all of us. The expansive energy, that creative engine – few of us are brave enough to feel it. Fewer still to act on it."

Starr left the great room and disappeared into the old sacristy. I could hear him climbing stairs that I never knew were there.

Within seconds, I heard the sound of the single church bell. It thundered as it tolled, telling the world Margaret Sedgwick was now beyond what any one of us could comprehend.

As the ringing of the last bell chimed a sinewy echo around the church, I thought about the writing consuming me, and the unknown, unexplored places it was taking me. I could see the manifestation of that story unfolding in glass, a resurrection of reverence that transcended anything we have ever created with our minds.

To understand what we did not know, but could perhaps feel the very edge of.

Starr returned from the sacristy stairs.

I walked over to the cerulean blue shard on the altar and held it up to the cross towering over Margaret Sedgwick. Through it, the colors comprising her name changed hue. They shone anew like her silvery blue eyes capturing the ever-shifting firelight.

"Cycles," I whispered, "connected through color, light, love."

I stood next to Starr and gave him the shard.

"When do we begin?" I asked.

Starr folded his fingers around the glass, a pulse of blue brought to life, and made the sign of the cross in alignment with the wooden marker over Megs' grave. The rosary shifted in the wind, as if receiving of the blessing.

"*Nunc*," he said, clutching the glass.

Right now.

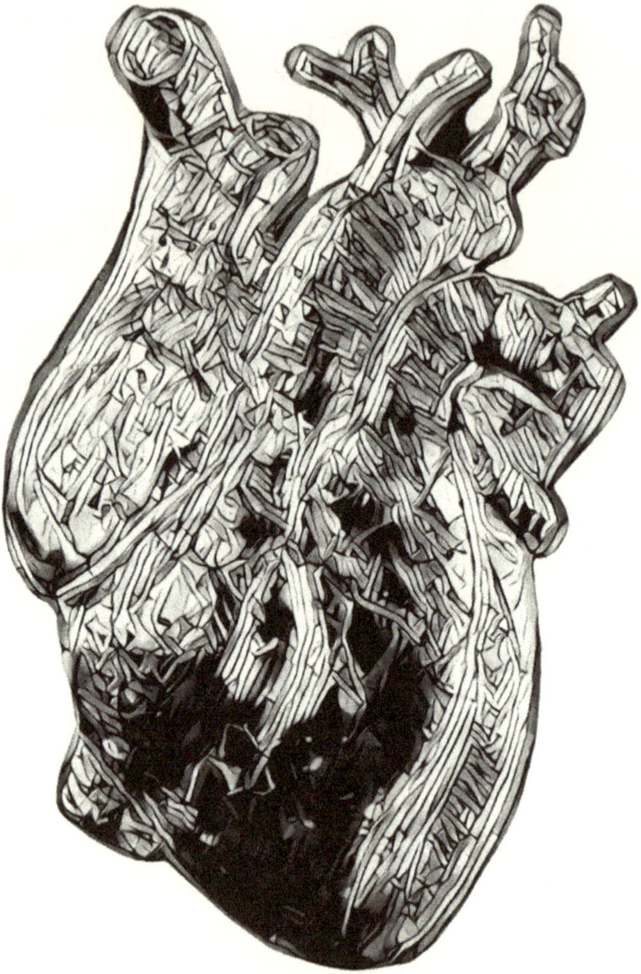

ABOUT RUS VANWESTERVELT

Rus is a writer and artist living in Towson, MD. He has been teaching high school and university students for 35 years, publishing his creative and journalistic work internationally. His most recently published novel, *Fossil Five*, is about a dying teacher and five of his former students, challenging readers to ponder the importance of the origins of love in the 21st century.

Rus earned his Master of Fine Arts in Creative Nonfiction from Goucher College, also in Towson, and currently mentors young writers in the art of the personal essay.

For more information, visit rusvanwestervelt.org.

ABOUT PRISMS & THE COLLAGE ESSAY

The Collage Essay has been called many things in its century-long existence. It has sometimes been referred to as a discontinuous, or patchwork essay; some authors even go so far as to call the collage essay a hybrid form of the lyric essay, which is when two or more stories are braided together for one greater theme or main point.

David Shields, in his book, *Reality Hunger*, defines the collage essay as "the art of reassembling fragments of preexisting images in such a way as to form a new image."

Prisms leans heavily on this definition, but I have added my own touch to this work. While most of the essay is completely true, I have taken the liberty to embellish, just a touch, here and there, to extend a greater truth to the overall meaning of this work.

Tim O'Brien, author of *The Things They Carried*, tells us that, sometimes, you have to lie to tell the truth. This is advice I took in crafting *Prisms*. To quote Kesey's Chief Bromden in *Cuckoo's Nest*, "Everything is true, even if it didn't happen."

And that's where we are.

I have retained the title "essay" in this work, simply because it is a compilation of very real shards of stories that have been reassembling into something very different in my life.

I imagine the same is true for you. We are all living a collage of memories, experiences, thoughts, nightmares, and celebrations that continue to contribute to the ever-evolving YOU in this present day.

For me, *Prisms* is where I am today. I know that if I were to write a similar essay in 15 years (God willing), it would look very different than this one.

There is such beauty in that transformation, that resurrection of shards of colored glass that we have been accumulating in our lives.

This essay would not have been possible without the courage and wisdom of my Collective partners, Jodi Cleghorn and Adam Byatt, and my closest life advisor, Jane Gordon.

This project started out as a social media post on my birthday in March: *56 things I've learned along the way.* It got such a strong response I considered publishing it as it was originally written. Conversations with Jodi, Adam, and Jane helped me realize the greater potential of the collage essay, a form I had only tinkered with in variations of the lyric essay. Like the very theme of the essay, the original concept shattered into a thousand pieces, and I accepted the challenge to recreate it, to become what it is here.

Do enjoy. I would love to hear from you after reading it, and I am always up for a good book club conversation, virtual or in person.

Feel free to reach out to me at rus@rusvanwestervelt.org.

as always.........................rvw | September 2021

THE JAR WRITERS' COLLECTIVE

The JAR Collective stands in the space of possibility between self-published indie author and micro press. Comprised of **J**odi Cleghorn, **A**dam Byatt and **R**us VanWestervelt, the collective harnesses the individual and collaborative passions, skill-sets and experience of the founding members to create an innovative publishing platform. The Collective consolidates more than a decade of creative synergy and shared relationships from author-editor and author-author to creative insurgents and catalysts, and a myriad of other transitory and permanent relationships between.

With JAR, you will not find work curated under a shared genre or form. You will find work offered from a shared passion for transformative stories in a kaleidoscope of forms. You can expect to find mainstream books offered alongside metaphysical digital serials, verse novels in chapbook form, black-out poetry and sci-fi constellation narratives, as solo and joint endeavors.

There are no limits here – no rules – and we invite you to join us in our explorations of the boundaries of narrative and shared literary adventures.

Join our email list at:
subscribepage.com/thejarwriterscollective

CPSIA information can be obtained
at www.ICGtesting.com
Printed in the USA
LVHW031652041221
705285LV00005B/132

9 780648 670643